Table of Contents

The Real Belle: How a Victorian Madam Became an Antebellum Icon
by Doug Tattershall

For Esther

With thanks to Jim Birchfield and all the staff at University of Kentucky Special Collections and the staff of the Lexington Public Library's Kentucky Room, not only for their help but for their dedication to preserving local history, and to Leslie Guttman, Joyce West, and the Carnegie Center for Literacy and Learning for their editorial assistance.

Belle Brezing in her private parlor, circa 1890

Chapter One

Belle Brezing waits for her guests inside her new house, a two-story, 26-room brick building at the corner of Megowan and Wilson streets. An orchestra warms up between potted palm trees, and a banquet table stretches the length of three parlors downstairs, set with red roses, linens, silver, cut glass, and china. Rows of numbered doors stretch the length of the back hall upstairs, also waiting.

Belle is a 29-year-old Victorian beauty. Round face with full cheeks, manicured eyebrows, a soft chin, and a broad forehead accentuated by hair swept up and back. Busty with a slender waist made more so by her corset. But standing erect with her chin up and dark eyes alert, she looks more the household general, which she is.

Guests arrive in horse-drawn buggy—doctors, lawyers, businessmen, and civic and social leaders in top hats and tails. They walk up the front steps and under an arch in the wooden box of spindles, lattice, carvings, and cornices that encloses the front porch of an otherwise plain brick edifice.

The guests arrive alone, their wives left at home. Girls from Memphis, Nashville, St. Louis, Louisville, and Cincinnati, some wearing their sorority pins, join Belle's regular girls to greet the men. This is opening night at Belle's new showplace brothel in Lexington, Kentucky.[1] The encore will continue almost nightly for 27 years and make Belle rich and famous.

The place is no mere whorehouse. Belle provides clients with lavish entertainment, imported champagne, choice wines, and whiskey drawn from spigots tapped into oak barrels. New clients do not just knock on the door. Known clients refer them. And they do not pay cash. Belle keeps a coded account book. She charges $5 for a visit to an upstairs room, five to 10 times the usual price.[2] Belle's girls stand out from the average prostitute. She has them in evening dresses and puts them on their best behavior—no smoking and no swearing.

"When you walk into Miss Belle's early in the evening, you would think you were in an embassy," John Coyne, a local bartender, says.[3]

During the day, Brezing travels to City National Bank in a carriage driven by a silk-hatted coachman and two matching bays. She keeps 10 to 15 girls in her house and $10,000 to $15,000 in her bank account.[4] She has a sharp business sense and a sharper tongue. Once while securing a loan, she promises to pay the money back within six months.

"Miss Belle, you don't have to pay us back so soon. Your credit is good," the loan officer says.

"I know. But I have it to spare. I forgot about the Baptist convention in town," she is said to answer.[5]

Life is more elegant at Belle's even when the men are gone. Trips to the local department stores after hours, where Belle sits in a chair and gives approval or disapproval as her girls try on dresses. Box seats at the horse races, with bets sent down by servant. Shows at the opera house, arriving in time to draw all eyes away from stage just before the lights go down.[6]

One Christmas morning, a musician living in a boarding house on the courthouse square arrives at Megowan and Wilson to carol Belle and her girls. Belle has hired him to sing in exchange for cash and breakfast. John Jacob Niles already is collecting folk songs from all over Kentucky and will go on to publish, compose, and record. He will perform at Carnegie Hall 20 years later and be called, "Dean of American Balladeers," but this morning he sings "O Come, O Come Emmanuel," "Silent Night," "Jesus, Jesus, Rest Your Head," and his own "Go 'Way from My Window" in Belle's brothel.

"Very pretty whores at breakfast (good table manners)," he notes. "Mrs. Belle said come back anytime."[7]

THE REAL BELLE: HOW A VICTORIAN MADAM BECAME AN ANTEBELLUM ICON

Belle is a successful madam even before her grand opening on Megowan. Too successful. During the previous decade, from 1881 to 1889, she operates from houses on North Upper Street near A. and M. State College. Brisk business draws the attention of the wrong people. Brezing must move, but business is not so good she can build a showplace on her own. She needs a patron.

William M. Singerly owns *The Philadelphia Record* and is president of that city's Chestnut Street National Bank and Chestnut Savings Fund and Trust Company as well as Singerly Pulp and Paper Mill. His father began Philadelphia's street railway system in 1858, and the younger Singerly makes his fortune managing it, expanding it, and raising the value of his father's stock to $750,000, which William inherits then sells for double the amount.

He is a widower and grandfather. For relaxation, he enjoys raising cows and sheep—Holsteins and Cotswolds—on a farm north of the city. He also enjoys trotting horses. He does business with Kentucky breeders and attends races at the trotting track on the outskirts of Lexington, with its crescent grandstand topped by six candy-striped spires. He meets Brezing, 28 years his junior.

Mr. Singerly loves building projects. He has built a new office for the Record—a six-story structure topped by a gothic iron tower—and a great barn of stone and brick on his farm. He is undertaking Philadelphia's largest building project yet, constructing what will be a thousand new houses.[8] And after Belle's eviction from North Upper in 1889, he helps build the South's finest brothel.

Rumor has it he provides $50,000 for the project.[9] Belle buys the house at Megowan and Wilson from an Irishman, Michael Foley, who runs a grocery store and raises a family a block away, on Corral Street. She adds to the back of the house to provide the hall of bedrooms upstairs and a ballroom, two private rooms, and a new kitchen and pantry downstairs.

Belle and Mr. Singerly share more than a common interest in Singerly's money and evening entertainment in Lexington. They are both self-made, they take a practical interest in politics, and they are loyal Democrats. Mr. Singerly supports Grover Cleveland's presidential campaigns and is a close personal friend. On election night, Belle's loyalties are clear. A crowd gathers at the Phoenix Hotel on Main Street, where election returns are reported by wire. Belle enters the hotel about 1 a.m., fashionably dressed as always, this night wearing a pretty hat with ostrich plumes. When she hears the election is going for Cleveland, she throws her hat on the floor and jumps on it in celebration.[10] Belle Brezing, a bastard child born near the rail yard, has the ear of the White House.

The success of Belle's brothel affords her the chance to travel, but during a trip to New York on Saturday, March 16, 1895, she receives a telegraph announcing what could be an end to her lavish lifestyle. A fire, started in her private quarters, has left much of her house in ruins.

No one knows how the fire starts, but it spreads to the abundant draperies in her parlor and soon moves up the steps to the attic and over the entire roof. About 15 women still asleep in the house just before noon are roused and rushed out without time to put on their clothes. One occupant remains. Flora Johnston screams for help from a third-floor window. Someone runs back into the house, pulls out a mattress, and lays it on the ground below the window, telling her to jump. Flora swings out the window, stands a moment on the sill, then drops. She lands on her back, badly hurt. A doctor tends to her in a house across the street, expecting her to die.

A set of diamonds on the third floor fares better. Someone yells to the firemen that they can find the jewels in a drawer. A fireman climbs a ladder into a third floor window and rescues them. Firemen fight the fire for an hour. By the time they have put it out, the upper stories are charred and the finery downstairs is waterlogged.

THE REAL BELLE: HOW A VICTORIAN MADAM BECAME AN ANTEBELLUM ICON

"Madam Belle Breezing's magnificent house on Megowan street is now a mass of scorched and water-soaked ruins," the *Press-Transcript* reports the next day.[11]

Belle sees to it the story does not end there. Armed with a $40,000 insurance policy, she responds by adding a full third floor to the house, including another back hall lined with more numbered doors. She expands her own chambers to include a second-floor sunroom off her private parlor. She sends engraved invitations to a new grand opening and invites madams from Louisville and Cincinnati to bring their girls. Belle's girls dress in white to stand apart from the others. The fire only makes the brothel grander.

Belle's house shines brightest in Lexington's red light district—it is among the first homes in the city to have electricity[12]—and while the city fathers intentionally place the district away from the center of town, it is a hub of activity. When the local state college wins a football game, students bring the celebration to Megowan. They hitch a mule to a cart and parade down the street with three students riding the mule, members of the band packing the cart, and a hundred or more students marching behind. Prostitutes line the sidewalks to cheer and applaud.

"But Miss Belle has little time for college boys. They do not have her kind of money," William H. Townsend, a law student, recalls.[13]

The same year Townsend finishes law school, and his days of celebrating victories on Megowan, another student arrives in town. He is not much for sports; his interest is writing. He takes a part-time job as a proofreader for the *Lexington Herald*, the morning newspaper on East Main, while studying English. He later covers the police beat for the afternoon paper, the *Lexington Leader* at Short and Market streets. His name is John Marsh.

When Marsh arrives in Lexington, Belle's brothel is in full swing. By the time he leaves after World War I, the very idea of a red light district has fallen out of favor and Belle has closed her house. She lives the remainder of her life in seclusion in the old mansion. Meanwhile, Marsh moves to Atlanta and marries an aspiring novelist named Margaret Mitchell.

Marsh provides financial stability and proofreading skills that prove essential to his wife's success with *Gone With the Wind*. He also provides a character. Mitchell knows the story she wants to tell and has acquaintances to draw on for all her characters, with one exception. She wants a prostitute in the story, a hardscrabble madam with some class to serve as a believable confidante to Rhett Butler. Marsh tells his wife about Brezing, the perfect prototype.

So almost two decades into her seclusion, in 1936, Belle Brezing enters the pages of a Pulitzer Prize-winning bestseller as Belle Watling. Back in Lexington, she is the talk of the town again. Marsh and Mitchell deny any connection between Brezing and Watling, but Brezing's fame does not depend on her connection to *Gone With the Wind*. When she dies in 1940, only months after *Gone With the Wind*'s release as a film, *Time* magazine eulogizes her as the madam of the "most orderly of disorderly houses," with no mention of her presence in the bestselling novel or the blockbuster movie. The *Time* obituary runs alongside those of Olympic gold medalist Billy Fisk, retired Encyclopaedia Britannica editor Franklin Henry Hooper, Harvard University geology professor emeritus John Eliot Wolf, and Walter P. Chrysler, founder of the Chrysler Corporation.[14]

Not bad for a girl born into poverty and shame.

Belle Brezing, about 8 years old

Chapter Two

Up the James River west of the Virginia Tidewater lies a piece of land no one wants, beyond the falls and therefore beyond the reach of shipping. The Monacan tribe abandons it in the 17th century, Huguenot refugees abandon it in the 18th century, and John Cox abandons it in the 19th. The veteran of the American Revolution arrives in Kentucky a generation after the age of land claims, when a man could build a cabin and plant a patch of corn to claim 400 acres. Kentucky is settled, and whole hierarchies have emerged to fit between the status of gentry and slave. Cox and his family settle on farmland near Clover Bottom, 25 miles south of Lexington near the Kentucky River, somewhere above slave but below gentry.

He lives about 40 years in Kentucky, his last spent with his first and sixth children, Rebecca and Elias, and a granddaughter named Sallie.[15] He does not live to see his illiterate granddaughter bear an illegitimate daughter, Hester, on March 2, 1852.[16]

Sallie moves to Lexington in 1854, near the rail yard on the west end, with her father and her shame, now 2.[17] A second illegitimate daughter is born June 11, 1860. Mary Belle, or just Belle.[18] The girls are pariahs. Mothers forbid their children to have anything to do with them, and few children disobey. Elias leaves his daughter and granddaughters, returning to work as a farmhand in Clover Bottom.[19]

But there is more afoot than Grandfather. Only days after Belle's scandalous birth, Southern Democrats look to another fatherless Lexingtonian—John C. Breckinridge, a former vice president who lost his father at age 2—to run as their presidential candidate against Democrat Stephen Douglas and Republican Abraham Lincoln.[20] The Civil War is coming.

THE REAL BELLE: HOW A VICTORIAN MADAM BECAME AN ANTEBELLUM ICON

Lexington is home to Kentucky's largest slave market, and although divided, the city's sympathies tend toward the Confederacy. Belle learns to crawl, then walk, then romp while her hometown changes hands between Confederate and Union troops.[21] The war leaves Lexington forever changed. Longtime residents of the frontier's first notable city still carry an image of Lexington as a new Athens—seat of the first university in the west, the first newspaper, the first masonic lodge, the first lending library; the first performance of a Beethoven symphony in America.[22] The Enlightenment, carried across the Atlantic and through the Cumberland Gap, reaches its westernmost point in the Kentucky Bluegrass. The city has come to expect great statesmen, men of letters, artists, and inventors from its numbers, but after the war, the city will never again achieve such greatness. Belle will benefit from the decline.

On December 16, 1861, Sallie Cox marries a German named George Brezing.[23] Belle is 1, Hester 9. The girls take their stepfather's name, and they become a shopkeeper's family, but the change gains them no respectability.

At first, they keep a beer saloon on Water Street, then Brezing rents a grocery store on Main from a carpenter named John Milbourn. George and Sallie take turns running the store. Both are drinkers, and they begin fighting after a few years.

"He is a man of disagreeable and bad temper drunk or sober," Susan Brock says. "I know they live very disagreeably together."

One day, Bettie Coons goes into the grocery store and sees George drunk. He throws a bottle at his wife.

"I was scared and did not stop to say what I came for, but ran away," Mrs. Coons says.

The girls are not sheltered from the violence.

"They have difficulties a good many times," Hester, now 13, says. "He hits her with his fist. I have seen him hit her with a chair. I have seen him draw a knife on my mother. It was a butcher knife. I saw him draw a pistol on her."

"I heard my mother say she would burn the house."

George is a binge drinker who might go two or three months sober then stay drunk for a week. He is a mean drunk. He has difficulties with his landlord, and they stop speaking to each other. Brezing builds another store across the street in the summer of 1865. Milbourn sees the couple one day in front of the new store.

"I hear them a-talking. She is standing in the partition door, she goes around to the door and I see him hit her and knock her up against the scales, and that is the end of that affair," Milbourn says.

About the same time, Sallie approaches two policemen on the streets near midnight and asks them to go to her house, saying her husband has been whipping her. They find the door locked and cannot get in. Sallie shows her friends bruises on her shoulder, elbow, and leg, and a cut on her hand.

George begins visiting Sarah Jackson's whorehouse and spends a good deal of time with Sue Cummings there. Meanwhile, Sallie has her own problems with drink and infidelity.

She walks the streets late at night with various men. She takes business to the whorehouse of a Mrs. James. She takes the proprietor of McGourke's Coffee House Saloon on Water Street to the backroom upstairs, a room with a mattress and no lights.

By March 1866, she is fed up with her marriage. She arrives at Cook's Beer Saloon with a friend. Another customer treats them to a beer, but it is just a start. Sallie drinks glass after glass until she scatters beer all over the saloon. People clear out, and Sallie leaves with her husband, but they return half an hour later. She continues drinking while George sits quietly in a chair. Sallie takes an apple from her pocket and throws it at him, giving him a bloody nose. Her friend picks up his hat and puts it on.

"I'm as drunk as hell and don't care who knows it, and I'm not afraid of any Dutchman that ever lived," Sallie says.

She dances a jig and sings her remarks to a tune, then stares at her husband. He continues to sit still and silent. She then runs up to him, shakes him, and strikes his head against the wall. She wipes the apple in his blood on the floor.

"Here is Dutchman's blood," she announces.

She files for divorce later that month.[24] Judge William Cassius Goodloe grants the divorce in June. Belle has just turned 6.

Cook's saloon sits on Mulberry Street, between Main and Water.[25] Water Street is the heart of the old Babylon Block, Lexington's antebellum red light district. The district is not as old as the first university, the first newspaper, the first masonic lodge, nor the first lending library, but prostitution is an established part of the city's heritage by the time Brezing is a girl. It flourishes during Reconstruction, as a city hailed "Athens of the West" takes on an appearance that is more Wild West. It becomes a city of more than 60 saloons and a city with a violent sense of justice. Residents watch public hangings from upper-story windows and rooftops near the jailhouse yard at Short and Limestone streets. It is a city where close placement of two political rivals' letter boxes in the Main Street post office leads to double murder, and a city with a police force too busy with public drunkenness, brawls, and robberies to spend time on prostitution.[26]

Four years after the Brezing divorce, on May 18, 1870, Sallie marries another man, a carriage painter named William McMeekin.[27] Belle and Hester take a new name. Belle turns 10 a few weeks later. Hester marries John "Pick" Norton, a painter, a year later in 1871 and starts a new life on the east end of Main, away from Belle, their mother, and their stepfather on West Short.

As a schoolgirl, Belle always has plenty of money and dresses well. Her mother is a seamstress. Belle as young as 8 can be seen in a colorful striped dress billowing over her knees from beneath a black, lace-frilled jacket, with a white lace collar protruding from the top. She wears flowers in her hair, dangling earrings, and eye paint.[28] Sallie sees Belle as a doll or a dress form, or perhaps she wants her daughter to grow up fast, which she does.

"We kids can't understand why our families won't let us have anything to do with her," Margaret Egbert, who goes to school with Belle, says.[29]

Belle finds friendship where she can and falls back on determination when she cannot. She learns defiance from her mother and refuses to do what everyone so clearly wants her to do: go away. If for no other reason than defiance, she succeeds at school, but she has more than defiance in her favor. She is a smart girl. She earns Rewards of Merit from her teachers.[30]

As a young girl, Belle attends Broadway Christian Church, but she later joins St. Paul Catholic Church with her mother, a born Catholic.[31] She meets another parishioner, Dionesio Mucci, an Italian who buys and sells hides and metal scraps at the corner of Main and Georgetown streets. The 36-year-old man ruins her at the age of 12, and Belle discovers a new way to make friends.[32] She writes a poem about it in the scrapbook Mucci gives her as a Valentine's Day gift:

> Sitting to night in my chamber, a school girl figure and lonely,
> I kiss the end of my finger, that and that only.
>
> Riveries rises from the smoky mouth. Memories conger surround me. Boys that are married or single. Gather around me. School boys in pentalets roumping, Boys that now are growing to be young lads, Boys that liked to be kissed, and like to give kisses.
>
> Kisses well I remember them: Those in the corner were fleetest: Sweet were those on the sly in the Dark were the sweetest. Girls are tender and gentle. To woo was allmost to

win them. They lips are good as ripe peaches and cream for
finger.

Girls are sometimes flirt, and coquettish; now catch and kiss
if you can sin: could I catch both—ah, wasn't I a happy Girl.

Boys is pretty and blooming sweetly, yea sweetness over thair

rest. Them I loved dearly and truly and the best.[33]

Classmate Willie Sutphin is one of those Belle loves dearly and truly, but even her friendships at school teach hard lessons. On a spring day in 1874 when Belle is 13, Willie is outside Dudley School on South Mill Street playing with a small pistol when his friend George Sharpe fires the gun in Willie's face. George kneels beside his friend begging him to stop crying and assuring him it was an accident. The police captain wires Willie's parents, both out of town, urging them to come home.[34] He dies two days later. George's father offers to pay for the funeral, but Willie's family declines.[35]

Belle finds other boys to befriend and becomes known around town for engaging in the "most mundane of sublunary pastimes."[36] By Belle's 15th birthday, the McMeekins have separated. William McMeekin boards on South Spring Street while Belle and her mother live together, back on West Main. Sallie lists herself in the city directory as *Mrs. S. McMeekin (widow).*[37]

While still 15, Belle becomes pregnant. She marries a cigar maker, James Kenney, on September 13, 1875, with their mothers signing as sureties due to her young age.[38] Few people in Lexington talk to Belle, but talking about Belle is quite another matter. The *Daily Press* covers the teenage marriage with nudges and winks:

"A marriage in high life is reported by Miss Belle Breezing and Mr. James Kinney. The ceremony was performed at the residence of the bride's mother. It was brief but most significant, and performed in a manner so touching that it drew tears from the eyes of those who witnessed it. La Belle Breezing is no more. She is now Mistress Kinney."[39]

Nine days later, there is more news.

Johnny Cook, who works with Belle's newlywed husband at Martin Straus's cigar shop on West Short, has lost out on Belle's affection. Their boss jokes with the boy. Johnny takes it with good humor but says he is leaving town for Cincinnati. Belle sends him a letter with a lock of her hair and a photograph of herself:

"Dear One: Here it is and I want you to write to me when you go and believe me your truly girl as every, send me yours and don't forget it eather,

Your darling

Belle"

She inscribes on the back of the photograph, "put this close to my heart." She also sends a note asking Johnny to get her derringer out of hock from the pawnbroker before he leaves.

"Dearest One: I will be down town at three o'clock look out for me. I will go to the office and by the store. Ma has come, have my pistol for me."

Johnny meets Belle and walks her home, but keeps the pistol. He goes to Garland's grocery nearby, at Main and Georgetown. He buys cigars and treats another customer to one, asking him to call on him in Cincinnati. He stops by Mucci's hide shop, across the street on the same corner, then takes an alleyway that runs behind Main to Belle's backyard. He opens her backyard gate, puts the derringer to his temple, and pulls the trigger.

A man is seen at the gate immediately after, and by the time a crowd begins to gather around the boy's body, the gate is closed and the pistol has been placed on his chest.

Johnny's stepfather arrives, as does Charles Gibson, a court magistrate. He impanels an impromptu jury and examines Johnny's pockets. The boy's mother arrives and wails over his body even as women in the crowd lead her away. The stepfather has the body put in a wagon and is on the way home when the coroner meets him, impanels another jury, and holds another inquest.[40] The coroner holds a more formal inquest the next morning. Belle swears the alleyway gate has been nailed shut for some time.

Belle goes to Johnny's house on North Broadway to see his body before the funeral. His mother looks on, prompting the girl to leave in a hurry. Soon after, she delivers a poem to the newspaper office on West Main about the boy who "killed hisself." She pens a brief note above the poem:

"Please

"put this in the Press and Dispatch if want pay, send me word

"oblige Belle Brezing."

With her note, she includes a common graveyard rhyme in nine stanzas, beginning with,

"His busy hands are folded,

His work on earth is done;

His trials all are ended,

His heavenly crown is won"

and ending,

"There on the shores eternal;

His spirit beckoning stands,

Still guiding on his loved one

To Join the heavenly bands."

"Thems my sentiments," she says.

The editors of the *Daily Press* do not like the hasty verdict of suicide, on account of the tampered evidence.

"The boy Kinney who married Belle Breezing was a fellow worker with Cook, but what his doings were during the day, our reporter so far, has not been able to ascertain," the newspaper reports.[41]

Belle's husband flees to Cincinnati, but all juries declare the death suicide. He eventually returns to Lexington, but never to his wife.

Months later, on March 14, 1876, Belle gives birth to a daughter, Daisy May Kenney. Belle, her mother, and the baby girl spend two months together in their home on West Main before Sallie dies of uterine cancer on May 19.[42] Belle buries her mother in Calvary Cemetery, the Catholic cemetery on the west edge of town. During the burial, their landlord sets all their furniture on the sidewalk and padlocks their door. Belle returns from her mother's burial to find herself locked out of her home. Lizzie Barnett, a neighbor on West Main, takes in Daisy.[43] Belle promises to pay for her daughter's care and boards nearby at Jefferson and Short streets. She turns 16 on June 11, 1876.

Belle Brezing is alone. Her childhood has taught her to keep the company of her own thoughts, her sister, reading, and those few friends she can find. Later, after Dionesio Mucci, she learns to gain the eye of the opposite sex. The later lesson makes her a welcome addition when she knocks on the door of Lexington's best whorehouse; the earlier lesson prepares her to succeed away from it.

Belle arrives at Jennie Hill's brothel on a Christmas Eve.[44] She has been on her own for years and is still a teenager. She has not gone far. The brothel is a couple of blocks from the house she was evicted from during her mother's burial, and Daisy and the Barnetts live four houses down.

There was little need for prostitution a century earlier, when pioneers established Lexington on the frontier. Women were needed for childbearing and as farmhands. But the city grows. Young women look to prostitution to rescue them from broken homes, low wages, and lack of work.[45] Men look to it for diversion, especially when in town as college students or for the races. Lexington's first red light district opens about 1810. The district shifts until it lands in the Babylon Block, which closes during Belle's childhood. The business scatters, in the case of Jennie Hill's, even to Main, in the childhood home of former first lady Mary Todd Lincoln.[46]

Belle aspires to more. In 1881 at the age of 21, she rents a house at 156 North Upper and sets out on her own, with carpet and rugs and curtains and fixtures plus furniture, including a parlor suite, four mattresses, and five sets of springs, not to mention quantities of vinegar bought every trip to the grocer.[47] Belle becomes a madam.

With a smaller house, she is a working madam, facing the same occupational hazards her girls face. As such, even her ample supply of vinegar is not enough to prevent a second pregnancy, this one only months after striking out on her own. Remedies abound for "producing the monthly flow" and removing the "obstruction" to regular cycles.[48] Instead, Belle gives birth to another daughter in her new brothel. The quandary of what to do with baby Belle resolves itself. She dies in infancy.[49]

Prostitution is Sallie Cox's legacy to her youngest daughter, but motherhood sets them apart. By marrying, Belle gives her first daughter legitimacy, and by giving her up to Lizzie Barnett, Belle assures Daisy will know nothing of drunken fights, broken furniture, or men brought home to mother's bed for business. Belle is protective of her surviving daughter. She says she would kill any man who ever took advantage of Daisy.

"She is filled with emotion when she says it," Blanche Patterson, one of Belle's girls, says.[50]

However, Daisy will need protecting all her life. When she starts school at age 6, her teacher realizes the girl is simple-minded. Daisy seems destined for the Eastern Lunatic Asylum on Fourth Street, but Brezing will not have it. Instead, she places her daughter under the care of the Sisters of Our Lady of Charity of the Good Shepherd. Daisy will spend her life in their hands, first at their orphanage and school near Newport. She visits her mother occasionally; Belle takes a suite at the Phoenix Hotel when her daughter returns to Lexington, so that she may never enter a brothel.[51] Once grown, Daisy moves to the nuns' institutions in Michigan, ending up at St. Joseph's Retreat in Dearborn. She is buried there in St. Hedwig Cemetery, years after Belle's death. Her lifelong care is paid for by her mother.[52]

Business is good, so Belle can afford it. She is the talk of the town again. She transforms prostitution in Lexington from mere sex trade to social club.

"A ball at Miss Belle Breezing's, which will come off during the races, will probably be pretty breezy, and the proprietress will be the Belle of the ball. A large attendance is anticipated. Our reporter will be provided with a telephone and telescope, and will take it in from the top of Morrison College," reports the *Lexington Transcript* in 1883, under the headline, "Bal de Demi-Monde."[53]

Life in the underworld becomes a place of formal attire, at least at Belle's. Billy Mabon, a bookkeeper at National Exchange Bank on West Main, lives down the street from the new brothel and makes his way over. He buys two bottles of wine and time with one of Belle's girls.[54] He later becomes more than a customer. He takes up residence with Belle while keeping his own address and continuing to run in good society around town. Their relationship has all the appearance of a romance. He calls her Kitten.[55]

Rumor has it Billy loses his bank job over his relationship with Belle. He works as an individual bookkeeper, then as a clerk for Lexington Brick Company on East Main, and finally as bookkeeper and cashier for Lexington Water Works Co. on East Main. Rumors arise that Billy's job again is at stake and that Belle has convinced C.H. Stoll to buy the company to protect her lover's job.[56] A couple years after Billy starts working for the Water Works, Stoll and a syndicate of local businessmen complete the purchase of a controlling interest in the company for $230,000. The old directors move out and Stoll and his partners move in. The newspaper reports that Billy, as well as the company's superintendent, will keep their jobs.[57]

Billy has a unique place in Belle's brothel. He accepts being No. 2 only when the wealthy William Singerly of Philadelphia arrives in town, knowing that Belle cares for him and is only nice to Mr. Singerly because he has money.[58]

"I always thought a steamboat captain was the most envied man in the world until I saw the 'Papa' at Belle's," James Tandy Ellis, who frequents Belle's as a college student, says. "The way he swaggers in makes him the Lord of creation."[59]

Belle can afford her own house now. She buys one several houses down at 194 North Upper.[60] Business is better. She develops a network of well-connected friends, not just Billy and Mr. Singerly, but judges and bankers and policemen and lawyers.

Not everyone is a friend, though. Belle is not the only madam operating on North Upper. Even Jennie Hill buys a house and relocates there for a time.[61] It is too much for the neighbors. On January 11, 1889, a petition is delivered to Edward L. Hutchison, the city's attorney:

"We, the undersigned citizens living on or near North Upper Street, in this city, most respectfully inform you that certain women whose names are given below, are conducting houses upon North Upper Street, of that class commonly known as 'houses of ill-fame,' and that these are especially so in this case, as they are located near a college of young men, an Industrial School for the training of poor young women, and two of the public schools of this city.

"We further state that these houses are on a public street leading to all of the institutions, and that they are almost surrounded by as good citizens as live in Lexington, and that these houses are damaging to their property.

"We do therefore most respectfully, but earnestly, ask that you may use every means granted to you as an officer of the law of this city to have these nuisances suppressed as speedily as practicable.

"The names of the parties conducting these houses and their numbers are as follows: Bell Brezing, No. 194; Lettie Powell, No. 196, and Molly Parker, No. 154."

Charles Chilton Moore is the first to sign the petition. He is joined by 31 others including the president of the College of the Bible, the president of Kentucky University, the superintendent of Public Schools, and a trustee of St. Paul's African Methodist Episcopal Church.[62] Mr. Moore's name atop such a list is unusual. He is Lexington's most notorious atheist, a man who abandoned his faith while debating a skeptical cousin. As a minister, he eventually baptizes the cousin, but the minister, at the end of a sermon one Sunday, closes his Bible, walks out of his church, and never returns.[63] His objection to brothels on North Upper is based on his zeal for social reform rather than any religious conviction.

The solution to the problem on North Upper is Megowan, four blocks east in a neighborhood called the Hill. The Hill has been the preferred red light district for some time. So the petition is more an inconvenience to Belle than a threat. And thanks to Mr. Singerly's patronage, it becomes an opportunity. The bal de demi-monde finds a new home, but first there is business to take care of. Belle announces in the *Leader* on June 16, 1889:

"As I am about to move from my present residence, I wish to have all my accounts settled at once. Those having bills against me please call and settle, and those owing me do the same. I am anxious to have all settled at once. BELLE BREEZING"[64]

Accounts are settled, and the party at Megowan and Wilson begins in 1890 with Belle's opening night.

Belle's house is part saloon, part dance hall, part social club, and part brothel. Men do not necessarily select a girl and go upstairs when they visit. Ernest Featherstone and his friends sometimes bring doves by Belle's after hunting. Her cook prepares them, and the men return later to have their dinner.[65]

Belle attributes her success to an ability to keep her right hand from seeing what her left hand is doing; to keep parties going without men knowing who is in the next room. Her job is part hostess and part schoolmarm as she keeps the good times from getting out of hand.

During business hours, she sits in a room behind the stairs reading, giving her a view of the side and front doors. She does not like trouble. So when a customer like Joe Maurey opens the door after hours and calls up to her with three others behind him, she is not happy.

"That's old Joe Maurey with that squeaky voice and a lead dollar. Don't let him in here," she calls down.

Other customers receive better treatment. When a trotting-horse man visits, a good spender from Wichita, Belle comes downstairs well dressed with a hand full of diamonds. The man orders a bottle of wine.

"Duplicate that order," she says. "Looks like we are going to get drunk, don't it."[66]

The trots provide her wealthiest clients. Allie Bonner, a Boston banker, leases Belle's house through the entire meet when he comes to Lexington for the races. One night, a local horseman, Warren Stoner, has an oyster feast at the Phoenix Hotel and calls Belle to let her know his party of nine is on the way. She tells Mr. Stoner the house is leased to Mr. Bonner, but he comes anyway. Belle does not yield. Mr. Stoner takes his party to Mollie Irvine's house nearby and leases it until Mr. Bonner leaves.[67]

The races are key to giving Belle a reputation well beyond Kentucky. When Joe Keith and a partner oversee the shipping of horses from

Elmendorf Farm on the Paris Pike to Argentina, their conversation about home in a Buenos Aires hotel lobby is interrupted by another man.

"What do you keep popping off about Lexington for? There is nothing there but the Phoenix Hotel, Garrett Wilson's livery stable, and Belle Brezing's whorehouse," the man tells them.[68]

When the military comes to Lexington in 1898 during the Spanish-American War, Belle's brothel becomes the unofficial headquarters for the officers and the envy of thousands of enlisted, who are not allowed.[69]

Such success allows her the occasional grand gesture. When the Protestant Infirmary a block away from Megowan on East Short Street, suffers fire damage, there is a public call for sheets. Belle buys all the linens in stock at a Main Street store and has them sent over, but a nurse refuses the gift when discovering the donor.[70] Despite such snubs, Belle's bal de demi-monde has all the appearance of a good time without regrets. Even the violence is fun. When the police are called to Belle's to break up a fight one night, Mr. Singerly tells the policemen to leave the two men to their fight. He promises to pay for any damage. The men proceed to do $10,000 in damage to the house, but they leave together, singing. Mr. Singerly pays for the repairs.[71]

Belle Brezing's sporting house for men, Megowan and Wilson, circa 1890

Chapter Three

Clara Kessler is 16. She's at home alone in Cincinnati when a peddler comes to her house selling lace and shawls. He compliments her beauty and asks if she would like to be in Belle Brezing's famous house. He tells her how much money she will make.

"Alright," Clara says.

A telegram arrives a few days later:

"Come at once. Belle Brezing."

Belle wires a train ticket from Cincinnati to Lexington. Clara uses it to travel to her new home on Megowan. The year is 1897. Peddlers travel far and wide propositioning girls like Clara, especially in the mountains. A man named Buzz Ray recruits locally, hanging out at the ice skating rink on West Fourth when it opens in 1906.[72]

Clara takes the name Sayre when a man named Ephraim Sayre takes a liking to her. He works as a bank clerk but is heir to a rich uncle with no children. Ephraim pays $24 a week for Clara's exclusive attention, but hope of marriage and wealth ends in the winter of 1900. He dies of pneumonia at the age of 36.[73]

Clara remains at Belle's brothel until another man takes a liking to her, a horseman named Clem Beachy. He needs a house where he can bring customers when they are in town. Clara rents a house on Short, around the corner from Belle's, and is in business for herself. Sixteen years after leaving Cincinnati, in 1913, Clara receives a marriage proposal. Mr. Beachy has bought an apple orchard in Washington and plans to retire after the next trotting meet. He wants to spend the rest of his life with Clara. They are engaged, but he falls ill during the meet. He too dies, from cirrhosis of the liver. Hope of marriage ends again, but not hope of wealth this time. Mr. Beachy leaves Clara all his money.[74]

Romance ends better for some of Belle's girls. Belle gives her girls one day off a week and lets them keep all money earned after $24 for room and board, towels, maid service, and laundry.[75] Most girls spend their nights off hopping the other houses on the Hill with their dates. Belle does not understand why they are so anxious to go courting during their time off work.

"These girls don't have any sense. Every one of them thinks she has to have a man to throw her money away on. Believe me, I never gave a man a nickel in my life. It has always been the other way with me—the men give me money," she says.[76]

However, sometimes they marry, and even settle in Lexington and raise families, living a life Belle herself hoped to live when she was 15.

Like Clara Sayre, Maude Blandin travels from another state to work for Belle. She works in a New York brothel and hears about Belle's mansion from her own madam. The Buffalo madam has met Belle at the races in Louisville and travels with her to Lexington for a visit before returning home. When Maude hears about the mansion, her madam arranges for her to come to the Hill.

Once there, she meets John J. Riley.[77] He is a man about Belle's age, also born into poverty and also a parishioner at St. Paul's. Unlike Belle, he uses politics to pull himself up, serving first as a magistrate and then police judge, but he supports Belle's profession as a customer.[78] Maude and Mr. Riley take a liking to each other. He moves her out of Belle's to a small whorehouse on Deweese Street, and later to a place they can share. They live together for years, unmarried. As if to make up for it, he eventually marries her three times: before a justice of the peace in 1908, in a civil ceremony in 1911, and at St. Peter Catholic Church in 1921.[79]

Romance ends worse for others.

Three o'clock on a Monday morning is a quiet time, even at Belle's. Ollie Broaddus and Debbie Harvey have a side room to themselves on the first floor at that time on July 10, 1911. Ollie and Debbie have been intimate since the week of Christmas. His father warns Belle that his son is dangerous when drunk, but Belle pays no attention to him.[80] The couple see each other once or twice a week. He is a 28-year-old bachelor who works as a butcher. She is 22, redheaded, well built, and good-natured, and has been one of Belle's girls since leaving her husband, a local barber. Ollie already has come and gone once Sunday night. When he returns early Monday morning, Belle and her housekeeper, Pearl Hughes, are the only other ones on the first floor. Debbie asks him what is the matter.

Ollie is drunk and has a habit of causing trouble when he visits Debbie. Shortly after the couple enter the side room, Belle hears Debbie screaming, "Come quick, Miss Belle, he's killing me!"

Belle rushes to the room and finds Ollie kneeling on top of Debbie and twisting a knife in her neck while she continues to scream, "He's killing me!" Belle implores Ollie to stop and grabs his coat collar. He leaps up and runs toward Belle, who runs upstairs to avoid attack. She orders the housekeeper to call the police.[81]

Ollie leaps through a window, cuts himself on a pane of glass, and leaves a trail of blood down Wilson, left on Short then right on Walnut Street, opposite the direction of his home on Virginia Avenue. Police find him but are convinced he has nothing to do with the murder, so they let him go. A city ambulance takes Debbie to St. Joseph Hospital on Second Street. She dies minutes after arrival.

Ollie hides in a slaughterhouse on the Frankfort Pike, but he calls police after meeting up with his father, brother, and a lawyer. Police arrive at the Lexington Commercial Club—his sister, Anna Broaddus, is treasurer—on Short and Upper and arrest him.

He is tried in October. Anna testifies that her brother has suffered from bouts of depression since he was 19 and has tried to take his life several times by taking poison. His father also has attempted suicide, trying to slit his own throat and ending up at Eastern Kentucky Lunatic Asylum, and his mother and a sister have been of unsound mind as well. Two doctors testify that Ollie Broaddus is insane. Dr. George P.

Sprague, superintendent of High Oaks Sanitarium on South Broadway, explains that Ollie's left ear is abnormal, indicating mental unbalance. A jury meets for 10 minutes and acquits him on the ground that he is of unsound mind. The judge commits Ollie to the local asylum. He escapes the hospital on January 10, 1912, and flees to the next county and then to Indiana. He returns home the next fall and remains at large, but his sister notifies the local saloons not to serve him liquor. At hearing this, he threatens to strike her with a rock, and the police are called.[82] The authorities return him to the hospital.

Eleven years before the murder, Joseph M. Deuel, a New York City magistrate, points southward to demonstrate that the Tammany Hall political machine has not done so bad for his city. He gathers crime statistics from 199 cities and finds three cities of "extreme wickedness." They are Norfolk, Virginia, Savannah, Georgia, and Lexington, Kentucky.[83]

The posturing of a Yankee politician puts no pressure on Lexington's red light district, but the murder of Debbie Harvey does. Talk of the murder is heard in all parts of Lexington. Even madams in the district are concerned. The Harvey murder follows a ten-month period when three other women are murdered in the district. Two of the men involved commit suicide, and the third man recovers and claims the woman shot him and then committed suicide herself.

"It doesn't seem to do much good to have these men arrested for making trouble because they come back and kill one of us and then are turned loose by the juries or courts," one madam says.[84]

Police and fire commissioners meet two days after the Harvey murder and say they are ready to take drastic measures, including prohibition of the sale of alcohol in the district. Mayor John Skain says he would not be surprised if the commission acted to close the district itself.

Evening dresses and all the parlor finery at Belle's cannot cover reality. Murder is the worst of it, but not the entirety of it. Practically all of Belle's girls have gonorrhea.[85] Some have worse, especially syphilis. The sophistication is a sham. What looks refined in the parlor as the evening begins, does not stand under scrutiny. Even Alice Elliott, who everyone says is educated, cannot live up to such a reputation.

"She has memorized some passages from books, but when she says, 'I seen' and 'I taken,' my ideal of an educated whore is smashed," Mr. Ellis, a customer in his college days, says.[86]

Little else in the parlor is sophisticated, either. Horse racing three seasons a year and Belle's $5 rate help maintain a reputation of one ongoing underworld ball, but the image of Belle's as a place beyond the reach of college boys comes ironically from those who go there as college boys. In fact, most customers in the parlor are teenagers from the university, and the music, dancing, and cocktails at Belle's only meet the definition of a ball in her underworld setting. The simple one-step dances that have become so popular easily accommodate a variety of suggestive wriggles, shakes, twists, and pumps in a place like Belle's.

"These dances are vile, vulgar and degrading to the extreme. Inflamed with liquor and aroused in passion by physical contact and suggestive movements of the body, the men and boys finish the night with the inmates in their rooms. The liquor and the dancing are the dangerous stimuli that make it almost certain that every caller will become a customer, even if his sole purpose at first is merely curiosity," critics of local prostitution conclude.[87]

Reaction to the Harvey murder includes an indictment against Belle. She is charged with selling liquor without a license, selling to a minor, and selling on Sunday, but nothing comes of the charges. It is her 15th indictment. Only her first, in 1882, is for operating a bawdy house, and on that, Gov. Luke P. Blackburn pardons her. The remainder are for nuisance, running a tippling house, and unlawful sale of liquor. Over the course of 30 years, she pays $928 in fines.[88]

In other words, she has little to fear from the courts, and she knows it. At one courtroom appearance, the judge begins by asking Belle her name.

"Well! You knew it very well last night," she says.[89]

However, public opinion is not so easily bought, and murder at Belle's brings the opposition out. The resolve of the police and fire commissioners two days after the murder quickly wanes, but a group of concerned citizens remains determined. They form a vice commission. City commissioners agree in 1914 to fund an investigation. The vice commission includes ministers and doctors, businessmen and academics, the chairwoman of the Kentucky Federation of Women's Clubs Department of Social Hygiene, and the vice president of the Orphans' Association. They are not prudes. They are progressives, and they have trained their eyes on the city's Fourth Ward, home to the red light district and to one third of the children in Lexington.

"The child is now the ward of the State," they assert. "This brings to the State a new responsibility."[90]

Their description of prostitution differs sharply from the happy memories of college alums and race fans come to town for a good time. A member of the commission finds one boy selling candy in a brothel. The boy's mother makes it fresh every day and sends him there to sell it. Another sees a prostitute kissing and fondling a 6-year-old girl. Schoolchildren know where the houses of prostitution are in their neighborhood and can point them out. Messenger boys direct customers to houses, and often go there themselves.

"Every boy in town knows; besides, I work in a grocery on Saturdays and run errands. I come down here on Saturdays," a 13-year-old boy says.[91]

There are almost 200 prostitutes working in Lexington, in 55 houses. Only half the houses are in the red light district. Waiters and others at local hotels, even policemen, are ready to help men find prostitutes.

"The customers in Lexington's houses of prostitution are, as a general rule, boys, students, laborers, clerks on small salaries, and strangers in the city. On Saturday and Sunday evenings Megowan street and the whole well-known vice district is crowded with groups of young men. They are often partially intoxicated and noisy," the commission reports.[92]

To Belle's house, wealthier patrons come in cabs and taxis. Madams pay cabmen for each customer they bring, generally from the front of hotels.

The vice commission recommends closing the red light district and criminalizing prostitution. The madams argue their business would scatter all over the city and make matters worse. City commissioners side with the vice commission.

"Commissioners pass anti-vice ordinances: redlight district will be abolished in short time," announces the *Lexington Leader*.

"Lexington's notorious 'redlight' district, which has been a plague spot on the city, must go. The City Fathers have so decreed."[93]

Local churches observe "Purity Sunday" to celebrate the decision.[94] Some of the prostitutes on the Hill move to Cincinnati, Louisville, and other nearby towns, but most stay put, including Belle. She is 54, and now officially running a criminal operation. Feeling her age, she begins to take morphine about this time. She struggles for more than a decade to stop taking the drug, going to Dr. Charles Nevitt's Elmwood Sanitarium on East Maxwell, where he gradually reduces her dosage. But the trips are part of a cycle rather than part of a solution. Belle is an addict.[95]

She also is a widow. During the course of the vice commission's investigation, on August 22, 1915, Belle's husband, James Kenney, dies of chronic nephritis. He has been working as a cigar maker and living with his sister and brother-in-law east of Lexington on the Richmond Pike.[96] Belle has not seen him since he left town nine days after their wedding, 40 years ago. In his place, she has had the company of Billy Mabon.

Then the death of Billy Mabon comes, on February 16, 1917.[97] His body lies in the parlor of his sister, Alice B. Morgan, on West Third Street. Mrs. Morgan invites Belle to say goodbye to the man she has been with since she opened her first brothel on Upper. Belle arrives heavily veiled to the Morgan home. Mrs. Morgan admits her into the parlor, giving Belle as much time alone as she wants. Billy's body is later taken away to Cincinnati for cremation.[98]

Belle keeps her brothel open in spite of Billy's death and the city's anti-vice ordinances. Convincing Belle to close her house would take an army.

The U.S. Army arrives on June 15, 1917.

Soldiers set up Camp Stanley on a farm west of Lexington on the Versailles Pike.[99] The city fathers have worked hard to entice soldiers to town, sending a portfolio to the Army with assurances that the city will accommodate the camp and reduce prostitution and the large number of saloons.[100]

Raymond B. Fosdick, the War Department's chairman of the Commission on Training Activities, immediately sees that the city has reneged on its promise to contain vice. So he is receptive when the local Commission on Social Hygiene asks the War Department to help enforce the as-yet-unenforced local vice ordinances. He sends secret agents to investigate. On their first day, they find 167 soldiers in the red light district, 16 of them drunk. They enter five brothels, including Belle's. She fares well in the report, but she is now operating her house at less than half its capacity.

"153 Megowan Street—Bell Breezings—Six inmates. Price of house $5. Moerlein's beer sold. Inmates dressed in fancy gowns. No soldiers admitted," the agents report.

The grand jury is in session and Lexington's madams are cautious.

"We were told to be careful till the jury quits," one madam says.

Beatrice Huston, who runs a house on West Fifth Street, claims to have police protection.

"The intimation was strong that the police have full knowledge of all that is going on. They can't help knowing," the agents say.

The city is teeming with recently-paid soldiers. Ice cream parlors are packed with soldiers and prostitutes. Streetwalkers order ice cream then stand near a window until soldiers come in to join them. They eat their ice cream then leave for a cheap hotel. Two regiments have received orders to move on to Hattiesburg, Mississippi, and soldiers are saying goodbye.

"Some of the boys about to leave expressed regret at leaving 'good old Lexington where a fellow can have fun,'" the agents say.[101]

In response to Commissioner Fosdick's report, Mayor James C. Rogers hires two Cincinnati detectives to evaluate the situation. They spend 12 days in Lexington and paint a different picture.

"Being strangers and men of good appearance, these detectives were able to obtain admission to a very limited number of places, always reporting that the houses they visited were quietly conducted and a constant lookout maintained for the police," the mayor says.

Commissioner of Public Safety George Land orders Police Chief Jere Reagan to investigate any suspicious houses.

"The police and detectives reported that they could find no disorderly houses in operation here. If such houses were doing business, they stated, it was being done so clandestinely and so quietly that the local police and detectives were unable to find it out," he says.[102]

Local officials assume the problem will go away when the Army vacates Camp Stanley on September 27, but the public learns of the

War Department's report and the unpersuasive response of the local police. First with the Vice Commission and now with the Commission on Social Hygiene, concerned citizens have gotten involved. A throng fills the Opera House for an anti-vice meeting on October 29, 1917, in spite of blustery wind and heavy rain, proclaiming, "the work for a clean Lexington would be started today." The crowd resolves to identify local officials who have not enforced the anti-vice ordinances and get rid of them.[103] An election is only days away, and Judge Riley, who has met his wife at Belle's, is among those on the ballot.

Among the speakers at the meeting is Father William Punch, whose parish of St. Peter's includes the Hill. He tells of attending five trials in which women are charged with keeping disorderly houses, and although all five seem to have clear evidence of guilt against them, none are convicted. In three cases, juries acquit. In two cases, Judge Riley dismisses charges. Father Punch says the law will be enforced in town when people want it enforced.[104]

Five days later, the police chief resigns.[105] An attempt to oust Judge Riley fails three days later when he wins re-election by an overwhelming majority, but the political fallout is enough for Belle. Brothels have been operating differently since the Army came to town, but Belle has never run a place of quiet deviancy, with secretive knocks on the door and eyes peering out from the side of closed curtains. The hullaballoo in the parlor rooms downstairs mean as much to her as the private vice upstairs. So she closes her brothel. The ball de demi-monde comes to an end. The city directory lists her mansion as vacant the following year.[106]

In reality, there are two residents in the Brezing mansion now: Belle and her housekeeper. All the other large brothels have closed, too. The business changes when confronted with the local anti-vice ordinances and political pressure to enforce it. New pressure comes with the Prohibition Amendment in 1919. Some prostitutes leave town, some start a new life in Lexington, some continue on as prostitutes. Belle stays put, sequestered in her house except when she goes to church or visits her sister.[107] At home, she has the company of her housekeeper, Pearl Hughes, and, at times, her sister. Hester is a widow now, and her two boys have grown and moved on, so she visits Belle at the old brothel.[108] Belle has wealth, but Hester has had a life of marriage and family, what Belle only tasted for nine days back in 1875.

Belle has the comfort of this bit of company for eight years, but as 1925 turns to 1926, Pearl is diagnosed with ovarian cancer. Then in February, Hester contracts pneumonia and myocarditis. She lives with her sister when she becomes too sick to care for herself.[109] She dies March 1 at St. Joseph Hospital.[110] Pearl dies at Belle's house on August 29.[111]

"Pink, don't drink shine. Pearl killed herself drinking shine," Belle tells her friend and former girl Pink Thomas.[112]

Belle lives alone for the first time since burying her mother and leaving her daughter with Lizzie Barnett, 51 years ago. She hoards her possessions and neglects her mansion. She is a recluse. The south side of the house collapses in 1932, and she considers moving to a small house she owns on Deweese, but the neighbors there—"a small delegation of negroes"—hear about it and complain to the city manager, Paul Morton. He sends Margaret Egbert, Belle's old school mate and now the city's first female police officer, to visit Belle. A housekeeper lets Officer Egbert in. She sees the parlor, with its mirrored walls. She sees white enameled beds in the back rooms. She sees the horn chairs, with horns from steer fashioned into the arms, legs, and backs, in Belle's sitting room, said to be a gift from a customer from Texas. And she sees Belle's bed—"big enough for six people to live in"—with matching oak dresser, washstand, and wardrobe. Belle lies in the big bed, reading her Bible. She tells Officer Egbert there is an attic full of books and vases given to her by admirers.[113]

Officer Egbert suggests that Belle could not possibly fit her furniture and all her books and vases into the house on Deweese. Belle agrees. She spends $2,500 on repairs and stays.

In August 1933, Belle believes she is near death. She wants someone from the university to go through her books. She asks Dr. Nevitt, who has continued to see Belle regularly since she developed her morphine addiction, to arrange it. He calls Bill Townsend. Two decades earlier, Townsend reveled on Megowan after football games, but he is now a lawyer and respected authority on Abraham Lincoln, on account of his book, *Lincoln and His Wife's Hometown*. He also is a member of a small group of book collectors that includes history professor Thomas Clark.

Mr. Townsend pulls into the history professor's driveway on Forest Park Road, a leafy neighborhood near campus. He honks and calls loud enough for neighbors to hear, "Would you like to go to a whorehouse?"

The two men drive to Belle's mansion, but by the time they arrive, she has taken another sinking spell.

"We saw neither her nor her library," Professor Clark recalls.[114]

He gets another chance to examine her books with Mr. Townsend and Winston Coleman, a construction contractor and avid collector of local history who starts the book group as a way to share the home brew he has been making in his basement since Prohibition.[115] Belle's new housekeeper ushers the men into the parlor. Dust covers the grand piano. Paintings have peeled and cracked. The red carpets have moth holes as big as dishpans. The grandfather clock is still. Belle comes downstairs and invites the men upstairs to the books. She is a thin, bent, white-haired old woman.

"But with strikingly serene features, gentle and refined in speech and manner. She wears a beautiful kimono of black watered silk, with pink bedroom slippers on her unusually small feet," Mr. Townsend recalls.

He lingers in the parlor while the others go upstairs. He finds two photo albums and looks inside. He comes upon a photograph of the very parlor in which he stands. All is fresh and glittering. There is the banquet table stretching the length of three rooms, set with red roses, linens, silver, cut glass, and china. There are the potted palm trees. Written beneath the picture: "My opening night."[116]

Mr. Townsend, an attorney with Stoll, Muir, Townsend & Park, also finds an old journal of accounts that includes an entry for his law partner's father. He slips it under his vest and joins the rest.

Professor Clark is unimpressed by what he calls a "small collection of miscellaneous books." He leaves with only Belle's scrapbook, Mucci's present to an adolescent girl, which she has filled over the years with fashion ads, newspaper clips, Valentines, photographs, and prayer cards.

Messrs. Townsend and Coleman are more impressed. The collection includes history, biography, and literature, including first editions by local novelists James Lane Allen and John Fox, Jr.

Mr. Townsend shares Belle's account book at the next meeting of the book collectors. Other members ask where and how he obtained it, but they receive no answer. The group then establishes its one and only rule—none may ask how or where a member has gotten a book. They also give their group a new name: The Book Thieves. He later gives one of Belle's books to Professor Clark, *Housekeeping in the Blue Grass: A New and Practical Cook Book: Containing Nearly a Thousand Recipes, Many of Them Tried and Known to be Valuable; Such as Have Been Used by the Best Housekeepers of Kentucky and Other States* published in 1875 by the Ladies of the Presbyterian Church in Paris, Kentucky. It ends up in the university library.

Looking back on the days of Lexington's red light district, one madam says, "The amateurs put us out of business."

She is wrong, unless she means the throng of residents who put pressure on government officials who were on the take. But she recognizes how society has changed since the district closed. As Belle says to her doctor, all it takes to get a man today is a car and a bottle of whiskey.[117]

Auction at Belle Brezing's house, August 1940

Chapter Four

John Marsh becomes a newsman while just a boy, visiting the Maysville Daily Bulletin to spend time with his father, the newspaper's editor. John is the only one of Millard Marsh's five children who has any interest in the place. As an adult, he believes old newsrooms like his father's foster better writing than the newer, more hygienic ones, recalling the Daily Bulletin as "crowded, cluttered, and dirty enough to produce genius, if my theory is correct."[118]

When John is only 8, his father dies of a heart attack. The boy's older sister goes to boarding school, his older brother goes to work, and John helps care for his younger brother and sister. Eight years later, he leaves his hometown on the Ohio River and travels 65 miles southwest to Lexington to attend State University of Kentucky. He rooms with his older brother, Henry, on East Maxwell Street and begins his newspaper career in earnest at the *Lexington Herald*.

Where Henry loves science, John loves words. Henry's studies prepare him for a career in ballistics and chemistry. John's favorite classes study Wordsworth, Bryon, Shelley, and Keats.[119] But there is more than a love for words behind his interest in writing.

"We're both interested in people," John's sister Frances says of herself and John.[120]

John Marsh's years in Lexington coincide with the heyday and demise of one of the city's most colorful people: Belle Brezing. He finishes his degree in 1916. He teaches English composition at the university and works for the *Lexington Leader* until September 1917, when he enlists in a local hospital unit organized for the war effort by David Barrow, a local doctor. The Army calls up the Barrow Unit in February 1918. While John serves in Army hospitals in England and France, he files reports to the *Leader*.[121]

He goes back to work at the afternoon newspaper after coming home the summer of 1919, but moves to Atlanta the following March. Atlanta is a city of 200,000—four times the size of Lexington, with four daily newspapers. He takes a job writing for the *Daily Georgian* and in September 1921 meets Margaret Mitchell. His former editor at the *Leader* offers $35 a week to return to Lexington, but at this point even the prospect of being the newsroom's highest-paid reporter is not enough to make him leave Atlanta. John Marsh has fallen in love.[122]

Miss Mitchell has fallen in love, too, but with the wrong man. She first knew Marsh's roommate, Red Upshaw, and prefers his rowdy nature to Marsh's reserve. Red and Peggy marry September 2, 1922, at her parents' house on Peachtree Street.[123] John is best man.

The newlyweds regret their marriage immediately. Red's rowdy nature includes drunkenness and abuse, and Peggy's effusiveness includes talking during their honeymoon about her romantic feelings for her first love, who died in the war. Red leaves Atlanta, and Peggy, three months later. John is there to comfort her. She divorces Upshaw a year-and-a-half later and marries John on July 4, 1925.

Marsh offers Mitchell stability she is not initially drawn to but will need to become a novelist. He works in the public relations department at Georgia Power, and when he receives a raise in 1926, she is able to quit her job at the *Atlanta Journal* and stay home. A car wreck months later injures her ankle and makes staying home compulsory rather than optional. Homebound with a cast and crutches, she begins writing *Gone With the Wind*. Marsh is as excited about the manuscript as Mitchell is. He serves as the novel's first editor, cheerleader, and taskmaster.[124] Once published, the public even speculates that a Georgia housewife could not possibly have written it, and some see Marsh as the more likely author. John scoffs at such talk.

"It will interest you to know that I am in distinguished company in such rumors, for other stories have credited the book to Peggy's father,

her brother, Sinclair Lewis and several other literary celebrities. No, a man who works as hard as I do at my own job doesn't have time to write 1037 page novels or to collaborate in them. I did help in the mechanics of getting the thing to press—proofreading, checking facts, etc.—but that was all," he tells his sister.[125]

With one notable exception.

As often happens when Mitchell writes of Scarlett O'Hara, the author has herself in mind as much as Scarlett when she writes, "Like most innocent and well-bred young women, she had a devouring curiosity about prostitutes."[126]

Mitchell has missed her opportunity for background on the prostitute she wants in her novel. While still at the *Journal*, another reporter is assigned to a story about a wealthy woman having her ashes scattered at sea. The dead woman's landlord tells the young reporter she has found a diary that reveals how her tenant made her fortune. She was a prostitute.

"Of course, the cub hadn't gotten the diary. I shrieked at the lost opportunity," Peggy tells her sister-in-law. "If I had been on the story I'd have been carried out dead before I'd have left without it."[127]

Instead, Mitchell's husband provides the missing piece, telling his wife about Belle Brezing. Mitchell researches the Lexington madam, and Belle Watling enters *Gone With the Wind*.

As the first person Scarlett recognizes when she returns to Atlanta, Belle provides a glimpse of the decay that has occurred since the Civil War began. She foreshadows the depths to which Scarlett will have to stoop to survive after the end of the old order. She provides the phony alibi to save Scarlett's husband, Frank Kennedy, and other Klansmen after a raid, making the elite of Atlanta beholden to Rhett, but by no means appreciative. And she gives Rhett a place to run when he needs to get away from Scarlett.

THE REAL BELLE: HOW A VICTORIAN MADAM BECAME AN ANTEBELLUM ICON

The similarities between Belle Watling and Belle Brezing are unmistakable. They operate elegant brothels bought with funds from rich patrons. They send engraved invitations to special events. They travel in style. They have children sent away to boarding schools. They offer donations to hospitals only to have their offers rejected. They are known for dying their hair red, a detail a colleague of Marsh's shares with Mitchell.[128] And of course, their names differ by only four letters.

Within a month of publication in 1936, *Gone With the Wind* becomes the bestselling book at Lexington's Morris Book Shop in the Union Station terminal on Main. It remains the local bestseller for 38 weeks.[129] The story of the "beautifully-smiling plantation" and the transformation of the heroine from a "pretty, spoiled, loving girl into a hard-headed, determined business woman" resonates with local readers. The book holds the top spot in Lexington even longer than it does nationwide.

Of particular interest is Belle Watling. People see the connection with Brezing immediately. John knows of questions about the connection from friends and family back in Kentucky and from letters directly asking him. Marsh and Mitchell deny any connection between Brezing and Watling, at least in public. Mitchell already has shared the fact she was researching the Lexington madam's life, in a letter to her sister-in-law while writing *Gone With the Wind*. Marsh only acknowledges telling his wife about Brezing in a speech years later at a reunion of the Barrow Unit.[130] Otherwise, they never waver, although denials do little to persuade folks in Lexington.

"It is inconceivable that anyone as smart as John Marsh, as alert and keenly interested in people and happenings as he is, should have attended college here four years and then worked for about that much longer as a reporter, when it was part of his job to know who was who—not only among the respectable folk but also among the shady or notorious characters who so frequently figure in news stories ... it is just impossible, they argue, even if he had never seen her," Joe Jordan, a columnist for the *Leader*, says.[131]

The differences between the two madams, as much as the similarities, make official denials prudent. Watling lives in the Old South sequestered to the pages of a book and later the flashing frames of a movie. Brezing is a contemporary, very much alive and a woman of means. Although she never acts against her appearance in *Gone With the Wind*, she could have. She is worth about $10,000,[132] and everyone in town is reading the book and recognizing Brezing's place in it.

Gone With the Wind would have resonated with Lexington readers even without the local connections. They still see Lexington as an essential Southern city, and embracing an immensely popular novel about the Old South is a way of demonstrating that fact.

"Against a vast background of details telling us of that period in the history of the south embracing the glorious ante-bellum days, the stirring times of the War Between the States and the terrible days of reconstruction, the author weaves a tale unexcelled for good entertainment and for excellent story-telling," begins the local review.[133]

Lexingtonians nurse a self-image of their city as the old intellectual hub still run by landed gentry with a drawl. They long for validation of that image by outsiders, especially as the self-image becomes less true and projected images from mass media become the ones that count. John Marsh and Belle Brezing allow people in Lexington to solidify their Southern credentials by hitching their hometown to a piece of popular culture.

If a popular book can help, a blockbuster movie can do even more. Two years later, Hollywood comes to Lexington for the filming of *Kentucky*, a color film made for top money and extended run with name actors. Locals are thrilled.

THE REAL BELLE: HOW A VICTORIAN MADAM BECAME AN ANTEBELLUM ICON

For the Hollywood premiere, producers bring to California a party of about 25 Kentuckians, including the governor and his family, the lieutenant governor, and the mayors of Louisville and Lexington. The governor sings "My Old Kentucky Home" in a local nightclub, and the song becomes the theme song of the premiere.

For Reid Wilson, mayor of Lexington, the trip to California comes immediately after trips to Philadelphia for the Army-Navy football game and Havana for a convention of the Municipal League.

"But Lexington looks mighty good to me," he assures his constituents on his return.[134]

Everyone from the mayor to the press to the local movie theater shill like horse traders.

"Great tradition has inspired a great picture ... and the romance of the Blue Grass lives in Technicolor," the Kentucky Theatre crows in its advertisement for the local premiere. "You'll be proud you live in the Blue Grass after seeing this great film ...!"

The movie tells a story of horse racing, a family feud, and romance. It is filmed entirely in Technicolor, still a novelty at the time, and for beauty shots makes full use of actress Loretta Young and the Bluegrass countryside. It is an attractive and popular film without a particularly probing storyline. Perfect for the locals.

"It is a picture in which all Kentuckians will be interested and of which all of them can be proud for, unlike so many pictures of localities, this is one which does not necessitate any protests. Furthermore, it may become a widely popular movie, spreading the name and fame of Kentucky and her thoroughbreds and sport of racing all over the world," the *Lexington Herald* proclaims.[135]

Kentucky becomes the most popular film ever shown in Lexington, but the record is broken little more than a year later. The film version of *Gone With the Wind* arrives at the whites-only Kentucky Theater on February 16, 1940. To celebrate, the Business Girls Department of the YWCA holds a costume ball in the YWCA gym on North Mill the day before the premiere, with awards for the best Scarlett and Rhett.[136] The movie screens three times a day for eight days, then twice a day for six more days. It becomes even more popular than *Kentucky*, with an attendance of 28,341, the entire adult white population of the city and then some.[137] Belle has made it to the silver screen.

Such big news in Lexington is of little consequence to Belle. She is dying.

Dr. Nevitt has diagnosed the source of her pain as uterine cancer. Upon hearing the diagnosis, she has her doctor call the pastor of St. Peter's, the parish church of the Hill. Father Joseph Klein arrives, and she makes her confession.[138]

Belle calls Dr. Nevitt four or five times a day for relief now. He has had permission from a narcotics inspector since 1925 to give her all she needs, but even daily morphine doses of 25 to 30 grams are not enough to ease the pain. He prescribes it, and she administers it. She does not want to see anyone and never talks to the doctor about her life.[139] Her banker, James McFarland, vice president of First National Bank & Trust Co. on Main, handles her financial affairs. When her account runs low, he opens her safe deposit box and sells stocks, bonds, or diamonds to replenish it. Emma Parker is Belle's housekeeper now, but unlike Pearl Hughes, she does not live at the dilapidated mansion on Megowan, now renamed Eastern Avenue. Emma lives on Wilson with her sister. Belle has lived alone for 14 years.[140]

Six months after *Gone With the Wind* comes to the Kentucky Theater, Dr. Nevitt calls Father Klein again. The priest arrives with his burse, oils, pyx, and stole. He administers last rites on August 10, 1940. Belle dies in the early hours of the next morning.

Father Klein will not allow a requiem Mass at his church and insists any graveside service be done quickly. Belle is buried the next day in the presence of the priest, her housemaid, and pallbearers provided by

Baker Funeral Home. A couple of women, her former girls, watch from a distance.[141] A spectacle is avoided. Or at least delayed.

A week after her burial, auctioneer Sam Downing runs an ad in the *Sunday Herald-Leader*: "Public auction to settle the estate of Belle Breazing, Thursday, August 22nd, 1940, at ten o'clock a.m. prompt, corner of North Eastern Avenue and Wilson Street, Lexington, Ky. Entire contents of building including large mirrors; famous horn suite furniture; cut-glass; silver; china; bric a brac of all kinds and other furniture. Also fifty-one pieces of jewelry consisting of a diamond necklace; diamond solitaire rings; diamond dinner rings; rings made of other precious stones; and other jewelry of gold and stones of many kinds."[142]

By 10 o'clock a.m. prompt, a mob has formed outside the old brothel to gawk and bid. Dishes, crystal, dresses, furniture, jewelry, and bric-a-brac from the era that gave us the word *bric-a-brac* wait in stacks inside. Belle's rosary ranks with cheap jewelry left behind years ago by her girls, now all thrown together into one box.[143] Elegance peeks through fallen plaster and rotting woodwork. The carved stairway in the foyer still impresses, taking three turns to reach the second floor. The ballroom still has its red wallpaper and mirrored ceiling, although the keys on the mechanical piano have yellowed. The racks in the wine room still stand, but empty. No one has been in these rooms for years.[144] Nor in the bedrooms that line the back hallways upstairs.

Not a bit of asphalt shows beneath the layer of straw hats and fedoras floating over the intersection outside Belle's mansion. Never before have so many people come at one time, not even when the house is fully occupied and open for business. The house looms over the crowd wrapped around it, just as it looms over the one-floor bungalows of the surrounding neighborhood.

"Lord God, look at them ladies going into that whorehouse," an old man says from a front porch nearby, where a neighbor takes the opportunity to sell Cokes in the summer heat.[145]

There is no room for the hundreds of potential buyers, so Downing steps onto the front porch to start the bidding. The iron fence around the house is bent and fallen. Once-painted brick and wood are bare. Weeds cover the yard. An ailanthus has volunteered from the foundation and grown up to the windows of the sunroom above the front porch, but the tree is too spindly to cast any shade on the auctioneer.[146]

The crowd includes the likes of Mildred Chandler[147]—now wife of a U.S. senator and Kentucky's first lady only a year earlier, having made the trip to California for the *Kentucky* premiere when her husband was governor—and lawyer Bernard T. Moynahan, who will become a federal judge under President Kennedy. Mr. Moynahan's aunt has him bring her to the auction. When he notices a man bidding high on a gold bracelet from the back of the crowd, he wonders to her why the man has not moved up front to see what he is bidding on.

"Don't worry, Bernard. He has seen that bracelet a lot of times," she says.[148]

The auction spans three days and raises $5,756, the price of a typical house.[149] Jewelry sells on day one, dresses on day two, and furniture on day three.[150] The big sellers the first day are two diamond rings, one selling for $600, the other for $550. A diamond necklace sells for $450. The "famous horn suite furniture," brought out the first day because of their notoriety, sells for $50.[151]

On day two, women parade down the street in old-fashioned dresses and hats as they buy them. The university theater department buys a lot of them.[152] Besse Barker, a high school teacher, does too. They go for 50 cents apiece or less. Mrs. Barker will lend them to the university for stage productions, but later stops because the students do not take care of them. She also buys the madam's bedroom slippers for five cents, right out from under her bed, as the auctioneer lets buyers come through the house 20 at a time.[153]

Regina McKinley, another schoolteacher, comes two days and buys a set of etched bar glasses and a glass jardiniere with lion-head handles and roses that light up with electric light. Fire Captain Ray Sharp buys a nickelodeon and finds $25 in nickels inside. Ben Yent, a local bookkeeper, buys most of the diamonds.[154] On the last day, Clara Sayre enters the house she had first entered 43 years ago when she was a 16-year-old girl from Cincinnati. She is now almost 60 and still living around the corner. She climbs upstairs to bid on her former boss's bedroom suite, a six-foot-tall walnut headboard with carved fleurs-de-lis, a matching footboard, and two matching dressers. She pays $1,600.

"I like it. I was with Miss Belle the day she bought it," she says.[155]

She buys it but apparently leaves it. Flora Hudson, who opens a boarding house for black residents in the old Brezing mansion, comes into possession of the bedroom suite. A local lawyer will buy it in 1987 from Mrs. Hudson's estate for more than eight times what Clara pays.[156]

With the auction over and the crowds gone, the mansion is quiet again. The end of Belle's sporting house for men is a sensation, just as its opening night 50 years earlier.

Belle's death only months after the film release of *Gone With the Wind* only revives questions about Belle Watling, and the need for more denials. So when Joe Jordan telegrams John Marsh after Belle's death to see if he can get a story about her role in *Gone With the Wind*, Marsh's reply is as brief as it is dishonest:

"Neither Belle Watling nor any other character in the book was taken from any real person. All are fictional creations and any similarity of names was accidental. My regards to the Leader folks = John Marsh."[157]

Even so, news of Belle's death spreads from Lexington, first to Louisville.

"I hope the soul of old Belle may land on the Island of Peace and greet her old friends again, but perhaps some voice will call out: 'Well, well, here comes old Belle, a burstin' into Hell,'" Mr. Ellis, now a writer for the *Louisville Times*, writes.[158]

From Louisville, news spreads farther, to *Time* magazine:

"Died. Belle Breazing, about 82, famed Kentucky bawd; in Lexington, Ky. Her plushy, luxuriant salon, famed for its influential patrons and for being the most orderly of disorderly houses, was closed by the U.S. Army in 1917, when Camp Stanley was set up on the outskirts of Lexington. Day after Miss Breazing's death, the Lexington *Herald* ran her obit on the front page. All copies were sold by 10 a.m., brought private speculators $1 apiece, provoked many a caustic phone call (Sample: 'Is it true that to get on the front page of the Herald one must operate a house of ill repute?')."[159]

Two months later, Margaret Mitchell visits Kentucky for the first time, getting together with her mother-in-law and sister-in-law the week after Thanksgiving in Maysville at the home of George and Anna Frank. She arrives with her husband on a rainy Tuesday and promises to stay until the sun shines, or Thursday at the latest. She talks of her husband's hometown and how well she knows it from the stories he's told over the years.

"I feel that I know every house on Forest Avenue," she says.

She talks about her work with the Atlanta Red Cross for the war relief effort, helping to make surgical dressings to send to Great Britain. When a news reporter brings up the recent death of Belle Brezing, she has less to say.

"To clear up a point that Belle Watling in the novel wasn't the Belle Breeze who died in Lexington recently, Miss Mitchell said that the name

THE REAL BELLE: HOW A VICTORIAN MADAM BECAME AN ANTEBELLUM ICON

Belle was common and that there were a number of 'ladies of that profession' in Atlanta," the *Daily Independent* reports.[160]

After their Maysville stay, Mitchell and Marsh take a one-car train from Cincinnati to Lexington to visit John's brother Ben on Delmar Avenue. They decline an invitation to an event at the university's Student Union, citing their brief stay and Mitchell's dislike for large crowds and public speaking.[161] So the famous author successfully avoids the subject of the famous madam during her one visit to the famous madam's hometown.

Just as Belle Brezing is born on the eve of war, she dies on the eve of war. The Battle of Britain rages across the Atlantic Ocean, and while World War II never marches through the streets of Lexington, it leaves the city changed again. Lexington continues to cling to an image of antebellum gentility while slowly conceding all to the American mainstream. Main Street decays as old estates become new subdivisions. IBM, Dixie Cup, and Square D arrive with the promise of a share in American prosperity. Montgomery Ward, McAlpin's, and J.C. Penney arrive in shopping malls to help complete the anonymity.

Belle's life spans the intermediate era between her hometown's auspicious beginnings and its full entry into the mainstream. Her success allows Lexingtonians to cling to the idea their city is still special, capable of creating characters who defy definition. It also reveals how outsider recognition becomes more and more important. By making her way into *Gone With the Wind*, Belle achieves that most American of ideals—celebrity—and begins her move from folk hero to brand. She validates what people in her hometown want to believe: that Lexington is simultaneously out-of-the-ordinary and all-American, and that there is no reason it cannot be both.

THE REAL BELLE: HOW A VICTORIAN MADAM BECAME AN ANTEBELLUM ICON

Belle Brezing in a black waistcoat

51

Chapter Five

Belle Brezing is an unlikely person to have a taste for literature or an attachment to place. Yet there she is, always in the hometown that rejected her. There she is learning to read when no one wants her at school. There she is finding a spot where she can keep an eye on the doors in order to read while business moves along in her brothel. There she is filling her attic with books, afraid to let them go and then afraid to leave them to chance when death approaches.

Her upbringing and her profession, the mentality of the Industrial Age and the call of westward expansion, ought to move her toward the pragmatic and wandering. Instead, she remains rooted and even bookish. Like the robed figures from her time depicting Lady Liberty or Columbia, Belle depicts, oddly enough, a city once heralded as a new Athens, the one pioneers and planters built on America's first frontier. She carves a life from what seems like nothing, she loves money and success and displays it well, but she also values the appearance of taste and intellectualism, all like her hometown in its early days.

That is not to say she is a woman out of her time. Photographed in her private parlor in 1890, she is surrounded by Victorian finery, all crystal and porcelain, drapery and tassels, she herself in a silk dressing gown.[162] She is no more a latter-day frontierswoman than she is a proto-suffragette. She is a Victorian. That is to say, she is sentimental. We see it in her teenage odes to kisses and to the dead Johnny Cook, who loses her hand to his rival, co-worker, and friend, James Kenney.

Even this sentimentalism emulates her hometown. Belle's note to Johnny ("Ma has come, have my pistol for me") and her published lament of his death ("Upon his brow so peaceful no earthly shadows rest") fit neatly alongside a local heritage of honor easily offended and rivalries quickly leading to bloodshed.

THE REAL BELLE: HOW A VICTORIAN MADAM BECAME AN ANTEBELLUM ICON

Belle arrives during America's Gilded Age, but Lexington's gild has tarnished. The intellectual energy of the pioneer town that introduced higher education and publishing to the land across the wilderness is spent, but countryside and collective memory still feed local nostalgia. Among Belle's books are the novels of an author raised on an estate outside Lexington—Scarlet Gate—who uses the old gentility as the basis for a writing career.

"The longer I live here, the better satisfied I am in having pitched my earthly camp-fire, gypsylike, on the edge of a town, keeping it on one side, and the green fields, lanes, and woods on the other. Each, in turn, is to me as a magnet to the needle. At times the needle of my nature points towards the country. On that side everything is poetry. I wander over field and forest, and through me runs a glad current of feeling that is like a clear brook across the meadows of May. At others the needle veers round, and I go to town—to the massed haunts of the highest animal and cannibal," the author, James Lane Allen, writes.[163]

The streets Belle calls home are surrounded by Allen's fields and forests, but she lives her life largely within a half-mile radius among the massed haunts of the highest animal. Given her means, she could move, but she stays. She even becomes one of the city's patrons; as soon as Belle goes out on her own as a madam, she becomes known as someone who can help.

"For every bad Miss Belle did, she did 500 good ones. There were a lot of poor people in that neighborhood, and she helped any of them. There was an awful lot of stuff went out that back door to them," the bartender John Coyne says.[164]

This altruism sets her apart from the great philanthropists of her day, not just because she distributes it from a brothel. Altruism is the mark of a good Victorian. Making loads of money is a virtue, but so is being generous with some of the excess. Belle's good works differ. She helps people, not causes, and the religion of her childhood exerts a surprising influence throughout her life.

Belle lives just 16 miles from the source of America's Second Great Awakening, the religious movement that spreads from Cane Ridge and makes evangelicalism the semi-official religion of the South. At the same time, she is born into agnosticism's greatest age, 25 years after Darwin steps onto the Galapagos Islands. This, too, reaches Lexington, especially in the person of her nemesis Charles Chilton Moore, the minister whose debate with his skeptical cousin ends in a draw, with the skeptic baptized and the minister abandoning his church.

In Belle's life, the debate between evangelicalism and agnosticism also ends in a draw. She chooses neither. She remains on her own and, when need arises, looks to her childhood religion, as scorned by freethinkers and evangelicals as she herself is. Catholicism influences a number of important decisions in her life: her decision not to divorce her husband of nine days, entrusting her daughter to nuns rather than the Eastern Lunatic Asylum, her refusal to get an abortion when she becomes pregnant a second time, despite the obvious business complications.

We do not know how Belle reconciles prostitution with her faith, or if she even tries. Nothing tells us, not her scrapbook, not the stories told by those who knew her, not the newspaper accounts. We do know that when she knocks on the door of Jennie Hill's bordello on Christmas Eve, no one else will have her. Born illegitimate, ravished at age 12, pregnant at 15, married then hastily abandoned, she quite possibly faces the choice of prostitution or starvation.

Lucy, Agatha, Winifred, Philomena, Agnes, some of the most popular names among Belle's Victorian peers. They recall holy women who give their lives rather than lose their purity. Their stories have a particular resonance among 19th century women, but Belle Brezing is no virgin martyr. On that Christmas Eve, she chooses survival. *Survival* is perhaps the word her early life most brings to mind, so that when she finally does more than survive—riding down Main Street in her carriage, with its silk-hatted coachman and two matching bays, on her way to grabbing the notice of a nation—another word comes to mind just as quickly: *victory*.

In victory, Belle becomes magnanimous more than altruistic. Victorian altruism gives men respectability. It validates their virtue and contributes to social well-being. Belle has no respectability, no virtue to validate, and first-hand experience of hopeless social decay and ill will. Her good works are quite simply acts of charity and evidence of a latent faith.

So when Commissioner Fosdick, the Commission on Social Hygiene, and Father Punch condemn vice in the city, Brezing's defiance ends. Her opposition differs now. It is the U.S. Army, the local political machine whose support she has been able to buy in the past, not to mention her parish priest. More important, her circumstances have changed. She is 57 and set for life. Billy Mabon is dead. She is not so much defeated as she is done.

That is to say, done with prostitution, but not done with living. Outings always have been well planned and strategic for Belle. Her contact with the world has had more to do with the world coming to her than her going out. If reclusive means a preference for staying at home, she has been reclusive much of her life, but when her house closes, reclusiveness takes on a new character. She has more time for introspection, more time for reading, more time to dwell on memories. She lives her last years not so much reclusive as cloistered.

We know little of what she accomplishes during these last years. We know she continues to help others, she reconciles with her sister, she reads the newspaper, her books, and the Bible. And when Dr. Nevitt pronounces she is dying, she seeks a priest.[165]

Belle Brezing becomes a folk hero in her hometown long before she dies. Since then, she has been the subject of plays, historic preservation movements, artworks, and an annual bed race. Her name has been on a light beer and a gay bar, a racehorse has been named for her, and her bedroom suite fetches $13,320 at auction 47 years after her death. Even into the 21st century, Paul Moss, a cemetery groundskeeper, tends her grave and personally pays for the flowers he leaves there. He feels called to.[166]

People do not remember Belle because she was a loose girl who fell into prostitution when things got desperate. They remember her because her childhood is tragic and her response to it is grand. Every chapter of her life surprises. When children shun her at school, we do not expect her to become an educated and literate woman. When an older man ravishes her, we do not expect her to marry a nice boy. When she knocks on the door of a brothel, we do not expect her to become a grande dame.

When things go bad for Belle, she always does better than expected. She has brains and determination, and despite the base nature of her upbringing and her livelihood, she appreciates the finer things. She laments the plight of her daughter and the loss of marriage and family. She has pity on others and helps them as she can. She has empathy and determination.

The final chapter of her life is no less a surprise. The same determination that made her a strong reader as a girl and an enterprising madam as a young woman makes her an exemplary penitent. It is impossible to imagine Belle summoning a priest without intending to bear all. For Belle, any other intent makes the summoning unnecessary. After her death, only Father Klein knows what she has confessed.

Belle Brezing is buried in a lot she bought in 1886, when she has risen out of her desperate childhood and can afford to move her mother's body to a more proper burial place. Belle continues to rise in wealth and fame for three more decades, and then in the quiet of her closed house, she continues to live. When undertakers finally lower her body into the ground, she joins six others in her lot. There is her mother, Sallie. She lies under the most ornate of the gravestones, a six-foot-tall obelisk inscribed, "Blessed are the pure in heart." There is Hester Norton, her sister. There is Pearl Hughes, her housekeeper. There are Rebecca Hall, who dies in 1887, and Sarah Denney, who dies in 1929, two more of

Belle's prostitutes. There is Simmie Culton, the son of Belle Campbell, known as Big Tit Lil when she worked at Belle's. Culton is a manic-depressive whom Belle takes in after he contracts tuberculosis. He dies of the disease in 1938 at the local asylum.[167]

Mary Belle Kenney assembles her own family at Calvary Cemetery, a makeshift one made up of people who enter her life and need her. She makes a name for herself, but the name is as illegitimate as she is. Although engraved on her tombstone, it is a name that has never really been hers: Belle Brezing.

[1] William Townsend, *The Most Orderly of Disorderly Houses* (Lexington: privately printed, 1966): 5-6.

[2] Blanche Patterson, interview with Joe Jordan, August 1941, Lexington, Kentucky, E.I. "Buddy" Thompson Papers, File 38-8, University of Kentucky Special Collections, Lexington, Kentucky.

[3] John Coyne, interview with Joe Jordan, 20 February 1956, Lexington, Kentucky, Thompson Papers, File 40-5.

[4] J. Winston Coleman, *Belle Breezing: A Famous Lexington Bawd* (New York: Winburn, 1980): 9-10.

[5] John Alexander, *Miss Belle: Lexington's Famous Madam Who Ran the "Most Orderly of Disorderly Houses"* (Lexington: Coleman Publications, 1983): 39.

[6] Buddy Thompson, *Madam Belle Brezing* (Lexington: Buggy Whip Press, 1983): 92-93.

[7] Ron Pen, *I Wonder as I Wander: The Life of John Jacob Niles* (Lexington: University Press of Kentucky, 2010): 44.

[8] "The Story of a Busy Life: William M. Singerly Nominated for Governor of Pennsylvania," *New York Times*, 28 June 1894: 1.

[9] William Townsend: 6.

[10] J.B. Moore, interview with Joe Jordan, 31 March 1941, Lexington, Kentucky, Thompson Papers, File 41-5.

[11] "Mass of Ruins: Is Madame Brezing's House on Megowan Street," *Press-Transcript*, 17 March 1895: 2.

[12] Buddy Thompson: 64.

[13] William Townsend: 1-2.

[14] "Milestones," *Time*, 26 August 1940: 56.

[15] Court Order, 2 December 1850, Order Book H, Page 450, Woodford County Courthouse, Versailles, Kentucky.

[16] *Kentucky Birth, Marriage and Death Records*, Microfilm Rolls 994027-994058, Kentucky Department for Libraries and Archives, Frankfort, Kentucky, Ancestry.com.

[17] 1860 Census, District 2, Fayette County, Kentucky, Microfilm Roll M653-365, page 288, Family History Library Film 803365, Ancestry.com.

[18] Notes from Brezing's Bible, Thompson Papers, File 40-4.

[19] 1870 Census, Clover Bottom, Woodford County, Kentucky, Microfilm Roll M593-504, page 460B, Image 344, Family History Library Film 552003, Ancestry.com.

[20] Frank Hopkins Heck, *Proud Kentuckian: John C. Breckinridge, 1821-1875* (Lexington: University Press of Kentucky, 1976): 84.

[21] Robert Peter, M.D., *History of Fayette County, Kentucky*, (Chicago: O.L. Baskin & Co., 1882) 452-469.

[22] J. Winston Coleman, *Squire's Sketches of Lexington* (Lexington: Henry Clay Press, 1972): 16, 20, 24, and 30.

[23] Geo. Brezing and S.A. Cocks, 16 December 1861, Marriage Book 3, pg. 152, Fayette County Clerk's Office, Lexington, Kentucky.

[24] *Sarah Brezing vs. George Brezing*, 31 March 1866, Fayette Circuit Court, Lexington, Kentucky, Kentucky Department for Libraries and Archives.

[25] *Williams' Lexington City Directory* (Lexington: Williams and Co., 1864): 119.

[26] John D. Wright, Jr., *Heart of the Bluegrass* (Lexington: Lexington-Fayette County Historic Commission, 1982): 132-133.

[27] Wm. S. McMeekin and Sallie Brezing, 18 May 1870, Jefferson County, Kentucky, *Kentucky, Marriages, 1785-1979*, FamilySearch (www.familysearch.org).

[28] "Belle Brezing, about Eight Years Old," photo, Belle Brezing Photographic Collection, 1868-1983, Kentucky Digital Library (http://kdl.kyvl.org).

[29] Margaret Egbert, interview with Burton Milward, 28 March 1940, Burton Milward File, University of Kentucky Special Collections, Lexington, Kentucky.

[30] Scrapbook, 1874, Thompson Papers, File 38-7.

[31] Pink Thomas (aka Mrs. Cox), interview with Joe Jordan, 31 March 1941, Lexington, Kentucky, Thompson Papers, File 40-2.

[32] Buddy Thompson: 22.

[33] Scrapbook.

[34] "A Probable Fatal Accident: A Little Boy Shoots His Playfellow with a Toy Pistol," *Lexington Daily Press*, 21 May 1874: 4.

[35] "Death of Willie Sutphin," *Lexington Daily Press*, 23 May 1874: 4

[36] "Post Mortem Affection: Belle Brezing Indites a Rhyming Obituary to her Dead Lover: Heaven, from a Worldly Point of View," *Lexington Daily Press*, 25 September 1875: 4.

[37] *Prather's Lexington City Directory* (Lexington: Transylvania Printing and Publishing Co., 1875 and 1876): 157.

[38] James Kenney and Mary Belle Breezing, 13 September 1875, Marriage Book 5, pg. 224, Fayette County Clerk's Office.

[39] *Lexington Daily Press*, 15 September 1875: 4.

[40] "Suicide or Murder: A Young Man is Found Dead, with a Pistol by his Side, in an Alley on Georgetown Street," *Lexington Daily Press*, 24 September 1875: 4.

[41] "Post Mortem Affection."

[42] Buddy Thompson. 35.

[43] Pink Thomas.

[44] Mrs. A.R. Musser, interview with Buddy Thompson, 24 July (unspecified year), Lexington, Kentucky, Thompson Papers, File 41-31.

[45] Jamie Hawks Pack, *The Fashion of a Madam: A Material Culture Analysis of Garments from the Belle Brezing Collection* (Lexington: University of Kentucky thesis, 1992): 11-18.

[46] John D. Wright, Jr.: 132-133.

[47] Buddy Thompson: 45-46.

[48] Janet Farrell Brodie, *Contraception and Abortion in Nineteenth-Century America* (Ithaca: Cornell University Press, 1994): 225.

[49] Belle Brezin burial record, Lexington Cemetery (www.lexcem.org).

[50] Blanche Patterson.

[51] Clara Sayre, interview with Joe Jordan, August 1941, Lexington, Kentucky, Thompson Papers, File 41-5.

[52] Buddy Thompson: 46.

[53] "Bal de Dem-Monde," *Lexington Daily Transcript*, 12 May 1883: 4

[54] Buddy Thompson: 70.

[55] Book inscription, Thompson Papers, File 38-8.

[56] Joe Keith, interview with Joe Jordan, 10 February 1956, Lexington, Kentucky, Thompson Papers, File 40-4.

[57] "Water Works: Formally Passes into Control of the New Local Syndicate: Payment of $230,000 in Cash Completes the Important Transaction: C.H. Stoll the New President," *Lexington Leader*, 13 November 1904: Section 2, Page 1.

[58] Note File No. 3, Thompson Papers, File 38-8.

[59] James Tandy Ellis, letter to Underwood, 14 August 1940, Ghent, Kentucky, Thompson Papers, File 40-4.

[60] Alice Jackson to Bell Brezing, 18 July 1883, Deed Book 68, page 189, Fayette County Clerk's Office.

[61] Matthew McNamara to Jennie Hill, 20 October 1884, Deed Book 71, page 43, Fayette County Clerk's Office.

[62] "Petition of Citizens: To Have Suppressed Certain 'Houses of Ill-Fame' on North Upper Street, in this City," *Lexington Daily Press*, 13 January 1889: 1.

[63] Charles Chilton Moore, *Behind the Bars: 31498* (Lexington: Bluegrass Printing Co., 1899): 72-80.

[64] *Kentucky Leader*, 16 June 1889: 5.

[65] Ernest Featherstone, undated notes by Joe Jordan, Thompson Papers, File 40-2.

[66] Pink Thomas.

[67] Phil T. Chinn, interview with Joe Jordan, 9 February 1956, Lexington, Kentucky, Thompson Papers, File 40-4.

[68] Joe Keith.

[69] Townsend: 3.

[70] Buddy Thompson: 115.

[71] Buddy Thompson: 89-90.

[72] Margaret Egbert.

[73] Certificate of Death, E.D. Sayre, Jr., *Kentucky Death Records, 1852-1910*, 16 March 1900, Roll 994027-994058, Kentucky Department for Libraries and Archives, Ancestry.com.

[74] Clara Sayre.

[75] Blanche Patterson.

[76] Note File No. 3.

[77] Clara Sayre.

[78] "Judge J.J. Riley Dies Suddenly," *Lexington Herald*, 12 June 1923: 1.

[79] "Evidence of Early Marriage Introduced in Contest of Will," *Lexington Leader*, 1 March 1951: 1.

[80] Margaret Egbert.

[81] "Ollie Broaddus Stabs Woman to Death in Resort," 10 July 1911: 1; "Insanity is the Broaddus Defense," 5 October 1911: 11; and "Family Fights for Broaddus," 6 October 1911: 9; *Lexington Leader*.

[82] "Oliver Broaddus is Captured: Man Who Killed Debbie Harvey and Who was Sent to State Hospital, is Recommitted," *Lexington Leader*, 30 October 1912: 2.

[83] "A Slander of Lexington," *The Morning Herald*, 1 December 1900: 2.

[84] Citizen, "Reduce Crime in Redlight District: 'Citizen' Makes Suggestions of Reforms Which Occur to Him Apropos of the Tragedy of

Monday: Only One Conviction for Several Affrays," *Lexington Leader*, 11 July 1911: 4.

[85] *Report of the Vice Commission of Lexington, Kentucky* (Lexington: J.L. Richardson & Co., 1915): 44.

[86] James Tandy Ellis.

[87] Vice Commission report: 16.

[88] Buddy Thompson: 192.

[89] John Alexander: 36.

[90] Vice Commission: 29.

[91] Vice Commission: 32.

[92] Vice Commission: 16.

[93] "Commisioners Pass Anti-Vice Ordinances," *Lexington Leader*, 26 November 1915: 1.

[94] James Duane Bolin, *Bossism and Reform in a Southern City: Lexington, Kentucky, 1880-1940* (Lexington: University Press of Kentucky, 2000): 68.

[95] Charles Nevitt.

[96] Certificate of Death, James Kenney, 22 August 1915, *Birth and Death Records: Lexington*, Microfilm Roll 7011804-7011813, Kentucky Department for Libraries and Archives, Ancestry.com.

[97] Note File No. 3.

[98] "William Mabon," *Lexington Leader*, 17 February 1917: 3.

[99] "Camp Stanley is Name Given by Williams," *Lexington Herald*, 15 June 1917: 6.

[100] James Duane Bolin: 68.

[101] "Report of Investigation by Federal Agents of Lexington Vice Conditions," *Lexington Leader*, 23 October 1917: 5.

[102] "Mayor, Safety Head and Chief of Police Talk: On Report of Vice Conditions as Alleged Here," *Lexington Leader*, 23 October 1917: 1.

[103] "Commercialized Vice in Lexington Must End: Leading Men and Women Put Strength in Plan," *Lexington Leader*, 30 October 1917: 1.

[104] "Let the Law be Enforced," *Lexington Leader*, 30 October 1917: 4.

[105] "Chief Reagan, Smarting under Criticism, Resigns," *Lexington Leader*, 4 November 1917: 1.

[106] *R.L. Polk & Co.'s Lexington City Directory* (Columbus: R.L. Polk & Co., 1919): 51.

[107] Margaret Egbert.

[108] Buddy Thompson: 131.

[109] Buddy Thompson: 131.

[110] Certificate of Death, Hester B. Norton, *Vital Statistics Original Death Certificates (1911-1955)*, 2 March 1926, Microfilm Roll 7016130-7041803, Kentucky Department for Libraries and Archives, Ancestry.com.

[111] Certificate of Death, Pearl Hughes, *Vital Statistics Original Death Certificates (1911-1955)*, 30 August 1926.

[112] Pink Thomas.

[113] Margaret Egbert.

[114] Thomas D. Clark, *My Century in History: Memoirs* (Lexington: University Press of Kentucky, 2006): 343-344.

[115] J. Winston Coleman, Jr., *The Book Thieves Club* (Lexington: The Winburn Press, 1983): 9-10.

[116] William Townsend: 4-6.

[117] Charles Nevitt.

[118] Marianne Walker, *Margaret Mitchell and John Marsh: The Love Story behind Gone With the Wind* (Atlanta: Peachtree Publishers, 1993): 39-41.

[119] Marianne Walker: 48.

[120] Marianne Walker: 41.

[121] Marianne Walker: 50.

[122] Marianne Walker: 15.

[123] Anne Edwards, *Road to Tara: The Life of Margaret Mitchell* (New Haven: Ticknor & Fields, 1983): 80-81.

[124] Anne Edwards: 89, 109, 117, 128-131, 134, and 140.

[125] Marianne Walker: 319.

[126] Margaret Mitchell, *Gone With the Wind* (New York: Scribner, 1964): 248.

[127] Marianne Walker: 143-144.

[128] Buddy Thompson: 4.

[129] *Lexington Leader*, 26 July 1936 through 11 April 1937: 5.

[130] Buddy Thompson: 4.

[131] Joe Jordan, radio script, 2 July 1953, Lexington, Kentucky, Thompson Papers, File 41-5.

[132] First and Final Settlement of Nolan Carter as Administrator of the Estate of Belle Breezing, 2 July 1941, Settlements of Executors, Administrators Etc., Book 41, page 93, Fayette County, Kentucky, Kentucky Department for Libraries and Archives.

[133] Elizabeth McLeod Steed, "Fine Novel of South: 'Gone With the Wind' Brings to Life Men and Women of Days of War Between the States," *Lexington Leader*, 2 August 1936: 5.

[134] "Kentucky Party Returns Home after Trip to Movie Capital," *Lexington Leader*, 23 December 1938: 12.

[135] "Kentucky in the Movies," *Lexington Herald*, 6 January 1939: 6.

[136] "'Gone With Wind' Costume Ball Planned," *Sunday Herald-Leader*, 4 February 1940: 30.

[137] "'Gone With The Wind' Sets All-Time Marks," *Sunday Herald-Leader*, 25 February 1940: 28.

[138] Buddy Thompson: 140.

[139] Charles Nevitt.

[140] Flora Hudson and daughter Ruth, interview with Buddy Thompson, 21 June 1983, Thompson Papers, File 41-3.

[141] Rodgers Baker, interview with Burton Milward, September 1971, Lexington, Kentucky, Thompson Papers, File 41-26.

[142] *Sunday Herald-Leader*, 18 August 1940: 17.

[143] Buddy Thompson: 151.

[144] "End Comes to Belle Breazing: Dies at Ornate Old Home in Lexington," *Lexington Herald*, 13 August 1940: 1.

[145] Mrs. Edward B. McKinley, interview with E.I. "Buddy" Thompson, 3 November 1981, Lexington, Kentucky, Thompson Papers, File 41-5.

[146] "Crowd Gathered for Auction of Brezing Furniture and Personal Memorabilia," 1940, photo, Belle Brezing Photographic Collection.

[147] Gano Lee, interview with Buddy Thompson, 8 July 1982, Lexington, Kentucky, Thompson Papers, File 41-5.

[148] Bernard T. Moynahan, interview with Buddy Thompson, 11 June 1982, Lexington, Kentucky, Thompson Papers, File 41-5.

[149] Belle Brezing estate settlement.

[150] Buddy Thompson: 165.

[151] "Two Diamond Rings Bring Good Prices," *Lexington Herald*, 23 August 1940: 8.

[152] Mrs. Edward B. McKinley.

[153] Mrs. J.R. Barker, interview with E.I. "Buddy" Thompson, undated, Lexington, Kentucky, Thompson Papers, File 41-28.

[154] Mrs. Edward B. McKinley.

[155] Clara Sayre.

[156] Bill Estep, "Brezing's Bed Sold for $13,230 at Estate Auction," *Lexington Herald-Leader*, 21 September 1987: A1.

[157] John Marsh telegram, undated, Thompson Papers, File 41-28.

[158] James Tandy Ellis.

[159] *Time*.

[160] Urith Lucas, "Margaret Mitchell Visits Here: Author of Gone With The Wind Arrives for First Visit in Husband's Home Town and Wants a Sample of Kentucky Sunshine," *Daily Independent*, 27 November 1940: 1.

[161] "'Gone With The Wind' Author, Husband are Visitors in City," *Lexington Herald*, 29 November 1940: 1-2.

[162] "Brezing in Her Private Parlor, 1890," photo, Belle Brezing Photographic Collection.

[163] James Lane Allen, *A Kentucky Cardinal* (New Haven: College and University Press, 1967) 46.

[164] John Coyne.

[165] Buddy Thompson: 140.

[166] "Ask Us: Answers to your burning questions," *Lexington Herald-Leader*, 1 December 2004: D1.

[167] Fran Borders, e-mail to author, 10 September 2013, Lexington, Kentucky.